USER'S GUIDE FOR DJI AIR 3

Revealing the Strategies, Tips and Tricks for Mastering the Drone

By

Kevin Editions

4

Table Of Contents

Introduction

Chapter 1: Getting Started
  Unboxing and Initial Setup

Chapter 2: Understanding Each Controls
  Functions of the Buttons and Joysticks
  Using the Smartphone App for Enhanced Control

Chapter 3: Pre-flight Checklist
  Safety Precautions and Guidelines
  Checking the Drone's Condition Before Flight

Chapter 4: Basic Flying Techniques
  Takeoff and Landing Procedures
  Hovering and Basic Maneuvers
  Adjusting Flight Modes for Different Scenarios

Chapter 5: Advanced Flight Modes
  ActiveTrack for Subject Tracking
  Waypoints for Automated Flight Paths
  QuickShot Modes for Creative Aerial Shots

Chapter 6: Capturing Photos and Videos
  Understanding Camera Settings
    Tips for Achieving Professional-Quality
Shots
  Using Intelligent Flight Modes for Cinematic
Effects

Chapter 7: Post-Flight Procedures
    Landing and Shutting Down the Drone
Safely
    Maintenance Tips for Prolonging the
Drone's Lifespan

Chapter 8: Troubleshooting and FAQs
  Answers to Frequently Asked Questions

Introduction

The DJI Air 3 drone is an advanced aerial photography and videography drone that combines the latest technology with simple design. With a vast range of features and capabilities, the Air 3 is truly unbeatable in terms of versatility and performance among other drones.

At its core, the DJI Air 3 has a dual-camera system which incorporates a conventional wide-angle camera as well as a medium-telephoto one. This unique arrangement enables users to take breathtaking aerial footage with unmatched resolution and sharpness. The wide-angle camera provides an equivalent field of view of 24 mm, ideal for capturing grand landscapes or expansive scenes. On the other hand, the medium-telephoto offers an equivalent field of view of 70 mm for closer shots and dramatic effects. Shooting pictures or amazing landscapes does not matter; this two-camera system will always make sure you get it right every time.

The DJI Air 3 besides its twin-camera set-up has other amazing facets. One of these is the superior obstacle sensing system with full omnidirectional array sensory operation for detection and avoidance of obstacles all around it enabling a safer, intuitive way of flying beyond expectations. As a result, you are able to keep up with recording great moments without having to worry about running into something.

Also, the DJI Air 3 has a long battery life that allows it to fly continuously for up to forty-six minutes. Thus maximizing your capture time while minimizing recharging intervals. The Air 3's lengthened battery life ensures that there is sufficient duration for obtaining perfect shots be it during short video or epic air panorama shooting.

In relation to performance, DJI Air 3 remains a class apart. It can go with a maximum speed of 47 mph on horizontal plane and fly within the range of 19 miles making it possible to cover long distances in minimal time. Whatever the case, whether you are following a fast subject or exploring remote wild territories, this amazing rate of speed and range makes Air 3 an ideal tool for capturing stunning aerial pictures.

However powerful its performance is and however advanced its features are, DJI Air 3 is extremely easy to fly. With its instinctive flight controls and smart automated functionalities; even an amateur pilot can master the basics about flying DJI Air 3. When taking off or landing or even winding through small spaces, Air 3's intuitive controls ensure that flying is pretty straightforward.

Chapter 1: Getting Started

Unboxing and Initial Setup

To unlock the full potential of the DJI Air 3 for capturing stunning aerial footage, unboxing and setting up is the first step. This includes carefully removing the drone from its packaging and charging its battery, installing propellers and then connecting the remote controller to the smartphone. The smoothness and success of each flight depend on these steps.

As one receives a DJI Air 3 drone, they are met by extremely well-designed and innovative packages that reflect this brand's outstanding quality. There is a strong feeling of enthusiasm as users open this slim tiny box carrying it's iconic DJI logo. When they remove the box cover, a number of accessories such as; drones themselves, remote controls, propeller blades, charging wires or cables of all kinds can be seen.

Charging the Battery

The battery for the Air 3 would have to be fully charged before taking off to prolong flight time and improve performance. Charging the battery is a simple process that can be completed with the help of an included charger and power cable. Just plug the charger into a power source, put the battery in a special charging port and after that, it will start charging. The LEDs on the charger will light up when it's charging showing how far it has gone; usually, charging takes one or two hours depending on how much energy was left in the battery.

Propellers installation

The propellers need to be installed properly so as to ensure stable and balanced flight of DJI Air 3 helicopter. Usually, you will find four propellers including two clockwise (CW) ones as well as two counterclockwise (CCW) ones in your drone package. When installing them for flights check each propeller closely for any wear or damage signs. These are steps that ought to be followed by individuals during the installation of their drones' propellers:

- The motor arms can be seen on the Air 3, which are marked by letters (e.g., A, B, C, D).
- Match each propeller to its respective motor arm while making sure that their turning

direction agrees with the markings on either one of them (CW or CCW).

- Attach each propeller to its proper motor arm by pushing it down and twisting it right till they get secured tightly.
- Continue doing this for all four propellers ensuring they are properly positioned and tightened so as not to become loose when flying.

Linking the Remote Controller and Smartphone

The DJI Air 3 drone is controlled through a remote controller that has an interface while the smartphone provides additional functions and live video streaming via DJI Fly app. To connect a remote controller with a smartphone here are some steps that should be followed:

- First, click on the remote controller's power key to switch it on.
- To switch on the DJI Air 3 drone, press its power button which is situated at the body of the drone.
- After that, open your smartphone's DJI Fly app and follow the instructions given in order to connect with your drone.

- Following that, users are able to access a lot of flight controls, camera settings and intelligent flight modes from inside their application interfaces.
- You should make sure that you have securely mounted your phone on the remote controller using this built-in holder for smartphones so as to ensure stable connection throughout your flight.

By following these steps, users can unbox and set up their new DJI Air 3 drones quickly and easily. Now that you have charged the battery, installed propellers and connected remote controller let us fly high.

Chapter 2: Understanding Each Controls

The remote controller is an indispensable part of this system as it acts as a command console and provides an interface for piloting and controlling various functionalities of airship. Constructed with precision in mind by considering ergonomics; intuitive controls within easy reach making photography videos easier than ever before while maintaining reliable wireless connection between ground-based RC and flying UAV system with modernized abilities for capturing exceptional aerial footage effortlessly with assurance.

Design and Ergonomics

The remote control of DJI Air 3 is designed with a smooth and ergonomic shape that matches the hands of users perfectly for a non-tiring and comfortable use over long periods. The remote's lightness is combined with its sturdiness, making it equally reliable for beginners as well as experienced pilots in terms of controlling the drone during flight and camera functions.

Control Layout

Remote controller layout has been created to offer easy access to essential flight controls and camera settings. Located at the center are two precision joysticks which enable users to navigate their drone through air with accuracy and swiftness. The joysticks are surrounded by various buttons and switches each having its own function such as takeoff/landing, return home, changing flight modes.

Built-in Display and Smartphone Integration

One key thing about the DJI Air 3 remote controller is the presence of an inbuilt display that shows real-time telemetry data, live video feed, and links you up to DJI Fly app even without using an external smartphone or tablet. This high-resolution screen presents clear images that enable users to keep track of flight parameters confidently while capturing magnificent shots from above.

There is also the inclusion of a smartphone holder that is built in a remote controller where customers would prefer to use their smartphones or tablets to control their flights. This gives access to more features and settings on the DJI Fly app like intelligent flight modes, camera controls and live streaming.

Connectivity and Range

The DJI Air 3 remote controller employs latest wireless technology which enables it establish a steady and dependable connection with the drone so as to ensure uninterrupted communication between them even at long distances. The remote controller uses a maximum control range of up to 10 kilometers (6.2 miles) and supports both 2.4 GHz and 5.8 GHz frequency bands, thereby endowing users with unprecedented freedom when it comes to navigating through skies as well as capturing breathtaking aerial views from almost anywhere.

Intelligent Flight Modes and Automation

In addition to manual flight controls, the DJI Air 3 remote controller offers a range of intelligent flight modes and automation features that make flying the drone easier and more enjoyable than ever before. These include:

- ActiveTrack: Allows users to track and follow a subject automatically, keeping it in the frame at all times.
- Waypoints: Enables users to plan and execute fully automated flight paths, ideal for capturing cinematic shots and complex aerial maneuvers.
- QuickShot: Offers a selection of pre-programmed flight patterns and camera movements, allowing users to capture stunning aerial footage with just a few taps.

Remote controller is an essential component of the DJI Air 3 drone, providing users with intuitive controls, reliable connectivity, and enhanced capabilities for capturing stunning aerial footage. With its ergonomic design, built-in display, smartphone integration, and intelligent flight modes, the remote controller offers users everything they need to unleash their creativity and explore the skies with confidence.

Functions of the Buttons and Joysticks

The functions of the buttons and joysticks on the DJI Air 3 remote controller are designed to provide users with precise control over the drone's flight and camera functions, as well as access to a range of intelligent features and settings. Each button and joystick serves a specific purpose, allowing users to navigate the drone through the air, capture stunning aerial footage, and unleash their creativity with ease and confidence.

Joysticks

Left Joystick (Throttle/Yaw)

- The left joystick, also known as the throttle/yaw joystick, controls the vertical movement (throttle) and rotation (yaw) of the drone.
- Pushing the joystick forward increases throttle, causing the drone to ascend, while pulling it backward decreases throttle, causing the drone to descend.
- Moving the joystick left or right rotates the drone clockwise or counterclockwise around its vertical axis (yaw), allowing users to change the drone's direction.

Right Joystick (Pitch/Roll)

- The right joystick, also known as the pitch/roll joystick, controls the forward/backward movement (pitch) and sideways movement (roll) of the drone.
- Pushing the joystick forward tilts the drone forward, causing it to move forward, while pulling it backward tilts the drone backward, causing it to move backward.
- Moving the joystick left or right tilts the drone sideways, causing it to move left or right (roll), respectively.

Buttons

Power Button

The power button turns the remote controller on and off, allowing users to control the drone's flight and camera functions.

Flight Mode Switch

The flight mode switch allows users to select different flight modes, such as Normal, Sport, and Tripod mode, each offering unique flight characteristics and performance.

Takeoff/Landing Button

The takeoff/landing button allows users to initiate automatic takeoff and landing procedures with a single press, making it easier to launch and land the drone safely.

Return to Home Button

The return to home button activates the drone's return to home (RTH) function, causing the drone to automatically fly back to its takeoff point and land safely in case of an emergency or signal loss.

Camera Capture Button

The camera capture button allows users to capture photos and videos using the drone's onboard camera, ensuring that they never miss a moment of their aerial adventures.

Intelligent Flight Mode Buttons

The intelligent flight mode buttons provide quick access to a range of intelligent flight modes, such as ActiveTrack, Waypoints, and QuickShot, allowing users to capture stunning aerial footage with ease.

Pause Button

The pause button allows users to temporarily pause the drone's flight and hold its position in the air, providing a momentary break to assess the surroundings or adjust camera settings.

Customizable Buttons

Some remote controllers feature customizable buttons that can be assigned to specific functions or shortcuts, allowing users to personalize their flight experience and streamline their workflow.

By mastering the functions of the buttons and joysticks on the DJI Air 3 remote controller, users can unlock the full potential of the drone and unleash their creativity in the skies. Whether navigating through tight spaces, capturing cinematic shots, or exploring new perspectives, the intuitive controls and intelligent features of the remote controller make every flight a memorable experience.

Using the Smartphone App for Enhanced Control

The smartphone app is a powerful tool that enhances the control and functionality of the DJI

Air 3 drone, providing users with a range of advanced features, settings, and capabilities. With the DJI Fly app installed on their smartphone or tablet, users can access real-time telemetry data, live video feed, intelligent flight modes, camera settings, and more, all from the palm of their hand. Let's explore how to use the smartphone app for enhanced control of the DJI Air 3 drone:

Real-Time Telemetry Data

The DJI Fly app provides users with real-time telemetry data about the drone's status, including altitude, distance, speed, battery level, and GPS signal strength. This information is displayed on the app's interface, allowing users to monitor the drone's performance and make informed decisions during flight.

Live Video Feed

One of the key features of the DJI Fly app is its ability to display a live video feed from the drone's onboard camera directly on the user's smartphone or tablet. This live video feed allows users to see exactly what the drone sees in real-time, enabling precise navigation, framing, and composition of shots.

Intelligent Flight Modes

The DJI Fly app offers a range of intelligent flight modes that allow users to capture stunning aerial footage with ease and precision. These modes include:

- ActiveTrack: Allows users to track and follow a subject automatically, keeping it in the frame at all times.
- Waypoints: Enables users to plan and execute fully automated flight paths, ideal for capturing cinematic shots and complex aerial maneuvers.
- QuickShot: Offers a selection of pre-programmed flight patterns and camera movements, allowing users to capture stunning aerial footage with just a few taps.

Camera Settings and Controls

The DJI Fly app provides users with full control over the drone's onboard camera settings, including resolution, frame rate, white balance, exposure, and more. Users can adjust these settings directly from the app's interface, allowing for precise customization of the camera's performance and image quality.

Flight Logs and Media Management

The DJI Fly app automatically logs flight data and saves captured photos and videos to the user's smartphone or tablet. Users can review their flight logs, view their captured media, and share their aerial adventures with friends and family directly from the app's interface.

Firmware Updates and Support

The DJI Fly app allows users to download and install firmware updates for the DJI Air 3 drone and its accessories directly from their smartphone or tablet. This ensures that users always have the latest features, performance enhancements, and bug fixes for their drone, ensuring optimal performance and reliability.

By leveraging the power of the DJI Fly app, users can take their control and creativity to new heights with the DJI Air 3 drone. Whether capturing epic aerial landscapes, tracking fast-moving subjects, or executing complex flight maneuvers, the smartphone app provides users with the tools and capabilities they need to achieve their aerial photography and videography goals with ease and confidence.

Chapter 3: Pre-flight Checklist

Safety Precautions and Guidelines

Safety is paramount when operating the DJI Air 3 drone, ensuring not only the well-being of the pilot and bystanders but also the integrity of the aircraft itself. By following a set of safety precautions and guidelines, users can mitigate risks and enjoy their aerial adventures responsibly. Let's explore some essential safety precautions and guidelines for operating the DJI Air 3 drone:

1. Familiarize Yourself with Local Regulations: Before flying the DJI Air 3 drone, it's essential to familiarize yourself with local regulations and airspace restrictions governing unmanned aerial vehicles (UAVs) in your area. This includes understanding where you can and cannot fly, as well as any required permits or licenses for commercial drone operations.

2. Conduct Pre-flight Inspections: Prior to each flight, thoroughly inspect the DJI Air 3 drone for

any signs of damage or wear. Check the propellers, motors, battery, and other components for integrity and proper functioning. Ensure that all screws and fasteners are securely tightened and that the battery is fully charged.

3. Choose a Safe Flying Location: Select a safe and suitable flying location for operating the DJI Air 3 drone, away from crowded areas, airports, and other restricted airspace. Avoid flying over people, vehicles, buildings, and sensitive infrastructure to minimize the risk of accidents or collisions.

4. Maintain Visual Line of Sight: Always maintain visual line of sight (VLOS) with the DJI Air 3 drone during flight, ensuring that you can see and avoid obstacles, other aircraft, and hazards in the surrounding environment. Avoid flying the drone beyond your line of sight or in adverse weather conditions that may impair visibility.

5. Check Weather Conditions: Check the weather forecast before flying the DJI Air 3 drone and avoid flying in high winds, rain, snow, fog, or other adverse weather conditions that may affect flight stability and safety. Be aware of changes in weather patterns during flight and be prepared to land the drone if conditions deteriorate.

6. Respect Privacy and Property: Respect the privacy and property rights of others when operating the DJI Air 3 drone, avoiding filming or photographing individuals without their consent and refraining from flying over private property without permission. Be mindful of your surroundings and avoid disturbing wildlife or natural habitats.

7. Maintain Safe Altitudes and Distances: Fly the DJI Air 3 drone at safe altitudes and distances from people, buildings, and other objects, ensuring that you have adequate clearance to maneuver and avoid collisions. Adhere to local regulations regarding maximum altitude and distance limits for UAV operations.

8. Be Prepared for Emergencies: Be prepared for emergencies and unexpected situations when operating the DJI Air 3 drone, including loss of GPS signal, low battery, signal interference, and equipment malfunctions. Familiarize yourself with emergency procedures and practice safe landing techniques in case of emergency.

9. Follow Manufacturer's Instructions: Follow the manufacturer's instructions and guidelines

provided in the DJI Air 3 user manual and on the official DJI website. Pay close attention to safety warnings, operating procedures, and maintenance recommendations to ensure safe and reliable operation of the drone.

By adhering to these safety precautions and guidelines, users can enjoy their aerial adventures with the DJI Air 3 drone responsibly and confidently, minimizing risks and ensuring a safe and enjoyable flying experience for themselves and others.

Checking the Drone's Condition Before Flight

Checking the condition of the DJI Air 3 drone before flight is essential to ensure safe and successful operations. By conducting a thorough pre-flight inspection, users can identify any potential issues or malfunctions and take corrective actions to mitigate risks and prevent accidents. Let's explore the key steps involved in checking the drone's condition before flight:

Visual Inspection

Start by visually inspecting the DJI Air 3 drone for any signs of damage, wear, or abnormalities. Check the drone's body, arms, propellers, motors, and landing gear for cracks, dents, scratches, or other visible damage that may affect its structural integrity or flight performance.

Propeller Inspection

Inspect each propeller of the DJI Air 3 drone for damage, deformation, or imbalance. Ensure that the propellers are securely fastened to the motor shafts and that there are no loose or missing screws. Rotate each propeller by hand to check for smooth and unrestricted movement.

Battery Inspection

Check the battery of the DJI Air 3 drone for any signs of damage, swelling, or leakage. Ensure that the battery contacts are clean and free of debris, and that the battery is securely inserted into the drone's battery compartment. Verify that the battery is fully charged and has sufficient power for the intended flight duration.

Connection Inspection

Inspect the connections and cables of the DJI Air 3 drone, including those between the drone and the remote controller, as well as any connected accessories such as smartphones or tablets. Ensure that all connections are secure and properly seated to prevent signal loss or interference during flight.

Sensor Calibration

Perform sensor calibration procedures as recommended by the manufacturer before each flight, especially if the drone has been transported or stored in a different location. Calibration helps ensure accurate sensor readings and optimal flight performance, particularly in GPS-reliant flight modes.

Firmware Update

Check for and install any available firmware updates for the DJI Air 3 drone and its accessories using the DJI Fly app or DJI Assistant software. Firmware updates may include performance enhancements, bug fixes, and new features that improve the drone's stability, reliability, and functionality.

GPS Signal Acquisition

Verify that the DJI Air 3 drone has acquired a stable GPS signal before takeoff, especially if flying in GPS-reliant flight modes such as Return to Home or ActiveTrack. Allow sufficient time for the drone to establish a strong GPS lock and confirm the accuracy of its position information.

Camera Functionality

Test the functionality of the DJI Air 3 drone's onboard camera by capturing test photos and videos, checking for proper exposure, focus, and image stabilization. Verify that the camera gimbal is stable and responsive to control inputs, and that the live video feed is streaming smoothly to the remote controller or smartphone.

Environmental Conditions

Assess environmental conditions such as weather, wind speed, and visibility before flight, and determine whether they are suitable for safe drone operations. Avoid flying the DJI Air 3 drone in adverse weather conditions or environments that may pose risks to the aircraft or its surroundings.

By following these steps to check the condition of the DJI Air 3 drone before flight, users can ensure that the aircraft is in optimal condition for safe and successful operations. Taking the time to conduct a thorough pre-flight inspection helps minimize risks and enhances the overall flying experience, allowing users to enjoy their aerial adventures with confidence and peace of mind.

Chapter 4: Basic Flying Techniques

Takeoff and Landing Procedures

Mastering the takeoff and landing procedures is essential for safe and successful flight operations with the DJI Air 3 drone. By following proper protocols and techniques, users can ensure smooth and controlled takeoffs and landings, minimizing the risk of accidents or damage to the aircraft. Let's explore the key steps involved in the takeoff and landing procedures:

Takeoff Procedures

1. Preparation: Before takeoff, ensure that the DJI Air 3 drone is powered on and that all pre-flight checks have been completed, including a visual inspection, battery check, and GPS signal acquisition.

2. Location Selection: Choose a suitable takeoff location that is free from obstacles, obstructions, and potential hazards, with sufficient space for the drone to ascend vertically without interference.

3. Clearance Check: Verify that there are no people, animals, vehicles, or objects in the immediate vicinity of the takeoff area, ensuring that the drone has a clear path for ascent.

4. Propeller Spin-Up: With the drone positioned on a level surface, initiate the propeller spin-up sequence by pressing the designated takeoff button on the remote controller or within the DJI Fly app.

5. Vertical Ascent: Once the propellers are spinning at full speed, gently increase the throttle using the left joystick to initiate a vertical ascent, allowing the drone to lift off the ground smoothly and steadily.

6. Stabilization: Maintain control of the drone's altitude and orientation as it ascends, using the right joystick to adjust pitch, roll, and yaw as needed to keep the aircraft stable and level.

7. **Flight Mode Selection**: Depending on the desired flight mode and maneuverability, adjust the flight mode switch on the remote controller to Normal, Sport, or Tripod mode to suit the current flying conditions and user preferences.

Landing Procedures

1. Preparation: Before landing, ensure that the DJI Air 3 drone has sufficient battery power remaining for a safe descent and landing, and that all flight parameters are within acceptable limits.

2. Location Selection: Choose a suitable landing area that is clear of obstacles, hazards, and potential obstructions, with sufficient space for the drone to descend vertically without interference.

3. Descent Initiation: Reduce the throttle gradually to initiate a controlled descent, allowing the drone to descend vertically towards the designated landing spot at a steady rate.

4. Altitude Monitoring: Monitor the drone's altitude and descent speed closely, adjusting the throttle as needed to maintain a smooth and controlled descent while avoiding sudden drops or impacts.

5. Approach Angle: Adjust the drone's pitch and orientation to align it with the landing spot, ensuring a gradual and controlled approach without drifting or veering off course.

6. Touchdown: Once the drone is positioned directly above the landing spot, continue to reduce

the throttle until the aircraft gently touches down on the ground or landing surface.

7. Power Down: After landing, deactivate the propellers and power down the DJI Air 3 drone by pressing the designated power button on the remote controller or within the DJI Fly app.

8. Post-Flight Inspection: Conduct a post-flight inspection of the drone to ensure that it is undamaged and in good condition, and address any issues or concerns before the next flight.

By following these steps for takeoff and landing procedures with the DJI Air 3 drone, users can ensure safe, smooth, and controlled flight operations, enhancing the overall flying experience and minimizing the risk of accidents or damage to the aircraft. Practicing these procedures regularly and adhering to safety guidelines will help users become proficient pilots and enjoy their aerial adventures with confidence and peace of mind.

Hovering and Basic Maneuvers

Mastering hovering and basic maneuvers is fundamental for effectively controlling the DJI Air 3 drone and capturing smooth and professional-looking aerial footage. Hovering, along with basic maneuvers such as ascending, descending, yawing, pitching, and rolling, allows users to maintain stability and control during flight, enabling them to navigate through various environments and capture dynamic shots with ease. Let's delve into the techniques and considerations for hovering and performing basic maneuvers with the DJI Air 3 drone:

Hovering Techniques

Hovering is the ability to maintain a stable position in the air without drifting or moving horizontally. It's an essential skill for capturing steady and well-framed shots, especially when filming stationary subjects or conducting precise maneuvers. Here's how to achieve and maintain a stable hover with the DJI Air 3 drone:

1. Altitude Control: Use the left joystick on the remote controller to adjust the throttle and maintain a constant altitude. Gentle adjustments may be necessary to counteract changes in wind speed or atmospheric conditions.

2. Orientation Control: Use the right joystick to make fine adjustments to the drone's orientation, ensuring that it remains level and upright during hovering. Avoid making sudden or abrupt movements that could disrupt the stability of the hover.

3. GPS Mode: Engage GPS mode on the DJI Air 3 drone to take advantage of its advanced positioning capabilities, which help maintain a precise and stable hover even in windy conditions or turbulent air.

4. Visual Feedback: Monitor the drone's position and orientation visually or through the live video feed on the remote controller or smartphone app, making adjustments as needed to maintain a stable hover.

Basic Maneuvers

Once users have mastered hovering, they can begin practicing basic maneuvers to navigate the DJI Air 3 drone through the air and capture dynamic aerial shots. Here are some essential maneuvers and techniques to explore:

1. Ascending and Descending: Use the left joystick to increase or decrease throttle and control the drone's vertical movement. Ascend gradually to gain altitude and descend smoothly to lower the drone to the desired altitude.

2. Yawing: Use the left joystick to control the drone's yaw, or rotation around its vertical axis. Yawing allows users to change the drone's direction or orientation while maintaining its position in the air.

3. Pitching: Use the right joystick to control the drone's pitch, or tilting movement along its lateral axis. Pitching allows users to move the drone forward or backward relative to its current orientation.

4. Rolling: Use the right joystick to control the drone's roll, or tilting movement along its longitudinal axis. Rolling allows users to move the drone sideways or laterally relative to its current orientation.

5. Combining Maneuvers: Practice combining different maneuvers, such as ascending while yawning or pitching while rolling, to create fluid

and dynamic flight patterns and capture diverse aerial footage.

Safety Considerations

While practicing hovering and basic maneuvers with the DJI Air 3 drone, it's essential to prioritize safety and follow best practices to minimize the risk of accidents or damage to the aircraft. Here are some safety considerations to keep in mind:

1. Maintain Visual Line of Sight: Always keep the drone within your line of sight during flight to monitor its position, orientation, and surroundings effectively.

2. Avoid Obstacles: Be mindful of obstacles, hazards, and other aircraft in the vicinity, and maintain a safe distance to prevent collisions or accidents.

3. Practice in Open Spaces: Practice hovering and basic maneuvers in open, unobstructed spaces free from obstacles or hazards, such as parks, fields, or designated drone flying areas.

4. Monitor Battery Level: Keep an eye on the drone's battery level and return to home (RTH)

function to ensure a safe landing before the battery becomes critically low.

5. Adhere to Regulations: Familiarize yourself with local regulations and airspace restrictions governing drone operations in your area, and adhere to them at all times to avoid legal issues or penalties.

By mastering hovering and basic maneuvers with the DJI Air 3 drone and prioritizing safety and best practices, users can unlock the full potential of their aircraft and capture stunning aerial footage with confidence and precision. Practice regularly, experiment with different flight patterns and techniques, and enjoy the exhilarating experience of piloting a high-performance drone through the skies.

Adjusting Flight Modes for Different Scenarios

Adjusting flight modes for different scenarios is crucial for maximizing the capabilities of the DJI Air 3 drone and achieving optimal performance and results in various situations. Flight modes offer users a range of features and settings tailored to specific needs and preferences, allowing them to customize their flying experience and adapt to different environments, conditions, and shooting scenarios. Let's explore how to adjust flight modes for different scenarios with the DJI Air 3 drone:

Understanding Flight Modes

Before adjusting flight modes, it's essential to understand the different flight modes available on the DJI Air 3 drone and their respective features and functions. Common flight modes include:

1. Normal Mode: Standard flight mode suitable for general flying and aerial photography. Offers a balance of stability, maneuverability, and performance for capturing a variety of shots.

2. Sport Mode: High-performance flight mode optimized for speed and agility. Ideal for capturing fast-moving subjects or executing dynamic flight maneuvers with precision and responsiveness.

3. Tripod Mode: Slow and stable flight mode designed for smooth and precise movements. Reduces the drone's maximum speed and

sensitivity to control inputs, allowing for precise framing and composition of shots.

4. Return to Home (RTH) Mode: Automated flight mode that triggers the drone to automatically return to its takeoff point and land safely in case of low battery, signal loss, or user command. Ensures the safe retrieval of the drone in emergency situations.

Adjusting Flight Modes

Once users understand the different flight modes available on the DJI Air 3 drone, they can adjust and customize these modes to suit their specific needs and preferences for different scenarios. Here are some tips for adjusting flight modes for different scenarios:

Aerial Photography and Videography

- For capturing cinematic aerial footage or still images, consider using Normal or Tripod mode to maintain stability and control while framing shots.
- Adjust camera settings such as resolution, frame rate, exposure, and white balance to

achieve the desired look and style for your aerial images and videos.

Action Sports and Dynamic Movement

- When capturing fast-moving subjects or dynamic action shots, switch to Sport mode to maximize speed, agility, and responsiveness.
- Increase frame rate and use burst mode or continuous shooting to capture fast-paced action with sharp and detailed images.

Scenic Landscapes and Panoramic Views

- For capturing scenic landscapes or panoramic views, consider using Tripod mode to achieve slow and stable movements for smooth and cinematic shots.
- Experiment with panoramic modes or intelligent flight modes such as Waypoints or ActiveTrack to capture expansive vistas or follow moving subjects with precision.

Indoor Flying and Tight Spaces

- In confined or indoor environments, switch to Tripod mode to reduce the drone's maximum speed and sensitivity to control inputs, allowing for precise and controlled movements.

- Enable obstacle avoidance sensors and obstacle detection features to help navigate through tight spaces and avoid collisions with obstacles or walls.

Safety and Compliance

- When flying in restricted or regulated airspace, ensure compliance with local regulations and airspace restrictions by adjusting flight modes and parameters as necessary.
- Activate safety features such as Return to Home (RTH) mode or geofencing to ensure safe and responsible flying practices and prevent accidents or incidents.

Experimentation and Practice

Adjusting flight modes for different scenarios with the DJI Air 3 drone requires experimentation, practice, and familiarity with the aircraft's capabilities and settings. Take the time to explore different flight modes, experiment with camera settings, and practice flying in various environments and conditions to develop confidence and proficiency as a drone pilot.

By understanding the different flight modes available on the DJI Air 3 drone and adjusting them accordingly for different scenarios, users can maximize the capabilities of their aircraft and achieve optimal performance and results in a variety of situations. Whether capturing cinematic aerial footage, tracking fast-moving subjects, or navigating through tight spaces, customizing flight modes allows users to adapt to different environments and shooting conditions with precision and confidence, unlocking new creative possibilities and enhancing the overall flying experience.

Chapter 5: Advanced Flight Modes

ActiveTrack for Subject Tracking

ActiveTrack is a powerful feature available on the DJI Air 3 drone that allows users to automatically track and follow subjects while capturing smooth and steady footage from the air. By leveraging advanced computer vision and artificial intelligence technology, ActiveTrack enables the drone to recognize and track subjects with precision, allowing users to focus on framing shots and capturing dynamic aerial footage without the need for manual piloting. Let's explore how to use ActiveTrack for subject tracking with the DJI Air 3 drone:

ActiveTrack is an intelligent flight mode that utilizes the drone's onboard camera and sensors to identify and track subjects in real time. By selecting a target subject through the DJI Fly app or remote controller, users can activate ActiveTrack and initiate automatic subject tracking, allowing the drone to follow the subject while maintaining a constant distance and perspective.

Key Features and Functions

ActiveTrack offers a range of features and functions designed to enhance subject tracking and improve the overall user experience. Some key features of ActiveTrack include:

1. Subject Recognition: ActiveTrack uses advanced computer vision algorithms to recognize and identify subjects in the drone's field of view, including people, vehicles, animals, and other objects.

2. Subject Tracking: Once a subject is selected, ActiveTrack automatically tracks and follows the subject's movements, adjusting the drone's position and orientation to keep the subject in the frame at all times.

3. Obstacle Avoidance: ActiveTrack incorporates obstacle avoidance technology to help the drone navigate around obstacles and avoid collisions while tracking subjects, ensuring safe and uninterrupted tracking even in complex environments.

4. Customizable Parameters: Users can customize various parameters and settings for ActiveTrack,

including tracking speed, distance, and altitude, allowing for greater flexibility and control over the tracking process.

5. Advanced Tracking Modes: ActiveTrack offers different tracking modes to suit various scenarios and shooting conditions, including Trace, Profile, and Spotlight modes, each offering unique perspectives and tracking behaviors.

How to Use ActiveTrack

Using ActiveTrack for subject tracking with the DJI Air 3 drone is straightforward and intuitive. Here's a step-by-step guide on how to use ActiveTrack:

1. Select Subject: Launch the DJI Fly app on your smartphone or tablet and activate the ActiveTrack feature. Use the app's interface to select the desired subject by drawing a box around it or tapping on it directly.

2. Confirm Selection: Once the subject is selected, confirm the selection and adjust any desired parameters or settings, such as tracking mode, speed, or distance.

3. Initiate Tracking: After confirming the selection, initiate ActiveTrack and observe as the drone begins tracking the subject automatically, adjusting its position and orientation to keep the subject in the frame.

4. Monitor Tracking: Monitor the tracking process through the live video feed on the DJI Fly app or remote controller, ensuring that the subject remains in the frame and that tracking is smooth and steady.

5. Adjust Settings: If necessary, adjust tracking settings or parameters during flight to optimize tracking performance and ensure smooth and accurate subject tracking.

6. End Tracking: Once tracking is complete, deactivate ActiveTrack and manually control the drone's movements or switch to another flight mode as needed.

Best Practices for ActiveTrack

To maximize the effectiveness and reliability of ActiveTrack for subject tracking with the DJI Air 3 drone, consider the following best practices:

1. Choose Suitable Subjects: Select subjects that are well-defined, distinguishable, and easily recognizable by the drone's camera to ensure accurate and reliable tracking.

2. Maintain Line of Sight: Maintain visual line of sight with the drone during ActiveTrack operation to monitor tracking performance and intervene if necessary to avoid obstacles or adjust tracking settings.

3. Avoid Complex Environments: Avoid tracking subjects in complex or cluttered environments with dense obstacles or varying lighting conditions, as these factors may affect tracking accuracy and performance.

4. Practice and Experiment: Practice using ActiveTrack in different scenarios and environments to familiarize yourself with its capabilities and limitations, and experiment with different tracking modes and settings to achieve desired results.

ActiveTrack is a versatile and powerful feature that enhances the capabilities of the DJI Air 3 drone for subject tracking and aerial videography. By leveraging advanced computer vision technology and intelligent tracking algorithms, ActiveTrack allows users to capture smooth and steady footage of moving subjects with ease and precision, unlocking new creative possibilities and enhancing the overall flying experience. By understanding how to use ActiveTrack effectively and following best practices for subject tracking, users can take their aerial videography to new heights and capture stunning footage with confidence and precision.

Waypoints for Automated Flight Paths

Waypoints is an advanced feature available on the DJI Air 3 drone that enables users to plan and execute automated flight paths with precision and ease. By defining a series of waypoints or points of interest on a map, users can create custom flight routes for the drone to follow autonomously, allowing for hands-free operation and precise control over the aircraft's trajectory and movements. Let's explore how to use Waypoints for automated flight paths with the DJI Air 3 drone:

Waypoints is a flight mode that allows users to create and customize automated flight paths for the

DJI Air 3 drone using the DJI Fly app or compatible remote controller. By specifying the coordinates and altitude of multiple waypoints on a map interface, users can define a custom flight route for the drone to follow, including waypoints for points of interest, key landmarks, or specific areas of focus.

Key Features and Functions:

Waypoints offers a range of features and functions designed to enhance the planning and execution of automated flight paths with the DJI Air 3 drone. Some key features of Waypoints include:

1. Custom Flight Routes: Users can create custom flight routes by defining multiple waypoints on a map interface, allowing for precise control over the drone's trajectory and movements during flight.

2. Altitude Adjustment: Waypoints allows users to specify the altitude of each waypoint, enabling the drone to maintain a consistent altitude throughout the flight path or vary altitude based on specific requirements or preferences.

3. Point of Interest (POI) Mode: Waypoints offers a Point of Interest mode that allows users to

54

designate a specific point of interest or subject for the drone to focus on during flight, ensuring smooth and accurate tracking and framing of the subject throughout the flight path.

4. Speed and Orientation Control: Users can adjust the speed and orientation of the drone at each waypoint, allowing for dynamic and fluid movement along the flight path and precise control over the drone's speed, direction, and orientation.

5. Advanced Planning Tools: Waypoints provides advanced planning tools and features, including the ability to save and edit flight routes, import/export waypoints, and simulate flight paths to preview and test routes before execution.

How to Use Waypoints

Using Waypoints for automated flight paths with the DJI Air 3 drone is straightforward and intuitive. Here's a step-by-step guide on how to use Waypoints:

1. Open the DJI Fly App: Launch the DJI Fly app on your smartphone or tablet and connect to the DJI Air 3 drone.

2. Enter Waypoints Mode: Navigate to the flight mode selection menu and select Waypoints mode to enter the Waypoints interface.

3. Define Waypoints: Use the map interface to define multiple waypoints by tapping on the desired locations on the map. Adjust the altitude, speed, and orientation of each waypoint as needed.

4. Customize Flight Path: Customize the flight path by adjusting the sequence and arrangement of waypoints, ensuring smooth and efficient navigation along the desired route.

5. Review and Confirm: Review the planned flight path and waypoints to ensure accuracy and completeness. Make any necessary adjustments or corrections before confirming and executing the flight path.

6. Execute Waypoints Flight: Once the flight path is confirmed, initiate the Waypoints flight mode to execute the automated flight path. Observe as the drone follows the predefined route, navigating between waypoints and capturing footage or performing tasks as specified.

Best Practices for Waypoints

To maximize the effectiveness and reliability of Waypoints for automated flight paths with the DJI Air 3 drone, consider the following best practices:

1. Plan Ahead: Take the time to plan and prepare your flight path in advance, considering factors such as terrain, obstacles, and points of interest along the route.

2. Test and Adjust: Test the flight path in simulation mode to preview and fine-tune the route before execution, ensuring smooth and accurate navigation between waypoints.

3. Monitor and Supervise: Maintain visual line of sight with the drone during Waypoints flight operations to monitor progress and intervene if necessary to avoid obstacles or adjust flight parameters.

4. Review and Analyze: After completing the flight path, review and analyze the footage or data captured during the flight to evaluate performance and identify areas for improvement.

Waypoints is a versatile and powerful feature that empowers users to plan and execute automated flight paths with precision and ease using the DJI Air 3 drone. By leveraging advanced planning tools and intuitive interfaces, users can create custom flight routes tailored to their specific needs and preferences, unlocking new creative possibilities and streamlining aerial operations. Whether capturing cinematic footage, conducting aerial surveys, or mapping terrain, Waypoints offers a flexible and efficient solution for automated flight control, enabling users to achieve stunning results with confidence and precision. By understanding how to use Waypoints effectively and following best practices for planning and execution, users can take their aerial photography and videography to new heights and capture dynamic and compelling content with ease and precision.

QuickShot Modes for Creative Aerial Shots

QuickShot modes are an innovative feature available on the DJI Air 3 drone that allows users to capture creative and dynamic aerial shots with ease and convenience. By activating QuickShot modes, users can access a variety of pre-programmed flight maneuvers and camera movements, enabling the drone to perform complex aerial maneuvers automatically while capturing smooth and professional-looking footage. Let's explore how to use QuickShot modes for creative aerial shots with the DJI Air 3 drone:

QuickShot modes are designed to simplify the process of capturing dynamic aerial shots by automating complex flight maneuvers and camera movements. Each QuickShot mode offers a unique set of predefined flight patterns and camera movements tailored to specific creative effects and shot types, allowing users to capture stunning aerial footage with minimal effort and expertise.

Key Features and Functions

QuickShot modes offer a range of features and functions designed to enhance the creative possibilities and versatility of aerial photography and videography with the DJI Air 3 drone. Some key features of QuickShot modes include:

1. Pre-Programmed Flight Maneuvers: QuickShot modes include a variety of pre-programmed flight maneuvers and camera movements, such as orbits, helixes, dronies, and rocket shots, designed to

capture dynamic and engaging aerial shots with ease.

2. Automated Execution: Once activated, QuickShot modes automate the execution of complex flight maneuvers and camera movements, allowing the drone to perform intricate aerial maneuvers while capturing smooth and steady footage without the need for manual piloting.

3. Real-Time Monitoring: Users can monitor the execution of QuickShot modes in real time through the live video feed on the DJI Fly app or remote controller, ensuring that shots are framed and captured accurately and that the drone remains within the desired parameters.

4. Customizable Settings: QuickShot modes offer customizable settings and parameters, allowing users to adjust the speed, altitude, and other parameters of the flight maneuvers and camera movements to suit their specific needs and preferences.

5. One-Touch Activation: QuickShot modes can be activated with a single touch or tap on the DJI Fly app or remote controller, making it easy and

convenient to access and use these creative features during flight.

How to Use QuickShot Modes

Using QuickShot modes for creative aerial shots with the DJI Air 3 drone is simple and intuitive. Here's a step-by-step guide on how to use QuickShot modes:

1. Launch the DJI Fly App: Open the DJI Fly app on your smartphone or tablet and connect to the DJI Air 3 drone.

2. Enter QuickShot Mode: Navigate to the QuickShot mode selection menu in the DJI Fly app and select the desired QuickShot mode from the available options, such as Circle, Helix, Dronie, or Rocket.

3. Select Subject: Choose the subject or point of interest that you want to capture in your QuickShot, either by tapping on it directly in the DJI Fly app or using the remote controller to manually position the drone.

4. Initiate QuickShot: Once the subject is selected, initiate the QuickShot mode by tapping the

corresponding button or icon in the DJI Fly app or remote controller interface.

5. Monitor Execution: Monitor the execution of the QuickShot mode in real time through the live video feed on the DJI Fly app or remote controller, ensuring that the drone captures smooth and steady footage while performing the predefined flight maneuvers and camera movements.

6. Review and Save: After completing the QuickShot, review the captured footage or images in the DJI Fly app and save or share your favorite shots with ease.

Best Practices for QuickShot Modes

To maximize the effectiveness and creativity of QuickShot modes for aerial photography and videography with the DJI Air 3 drone, consider the following best practices:

1. Choose Suitable Subjects: Select subjects or points of interest that are well-defined, distinguishable, and visually appealing to ensure compelling and engaging shots.

2. Experiment with Settings: Experiment with different settings and parameters for QuickShot modes, such as speed, altitude, and orientation, to achieve unique and creative effects and perspectives.

3. Plan and Prepare: Take the time to plan and prepare your QuickShot sequences in advance, considering factors such as lighting, composition, and framing to ensure optimal results.

4. Monitor Performance: Monitor the performance of QuickShot modes in real time through the live video feed on the DJI Fly app or remote controller, making adjustments as needed to ensure smooth and accurate execution.

5. Practice and Refine: Practice using QuickShot modes regularly to familiarize yourself with their capabilities and limitations, and refine your techniques to achieve increasingly creative and compelling shots.

QuickShot modes are a versatile and powerful feature that empowers users to capture creative and dynamic aerial shots with ease and convenience using the DJI Air 3 drone. By leveraging pre-programmed flight maneuvers and camera movements, QuickShot modes automate the process of capturing stunning aerial footage, allowing users to focus on framing shots and capturing compelling content without the need for manual piloting. Whether capturing cinematic orbits, dramatic dronies, or breathtaking helixes, QuickShot modes offer a convenient and accessible solution for achieving professional-quality aerial shots with minimal effort and expertise. By understanding how to use QuickShot modes effectively

Chapter 6: Capturing Photos and Videos

Understanding Camera Settings

Understanding camera settings is essential for maximizing the capabilities of the DJI Air 3 drone and achieving optimal results in aerial photography and videography. By familiarizing yourself with the various camera settings available on the drone, you can customize your shooting experience, adjust image quality, and capture stunning footage tailored to your specific needs and preferences. Let's explore the key camera settings and how to use them effectively:

Resolution and Aspect Ratio

The resolution setting determines the number of pixels in each frame of your footage or image. Higher resolutions offer greater detail and clarity but may require more storage space. The DJI Air 3 drone offers various resolution options, including 4K and Full HD, allowing you to choose the appropriate resolution for your project. Additionally, you can adjust the aspect ratio to control the dimensions of your images or videos, such as 16:9 for widescreen or 4:3 for standard.

Frame Rate

The frame rate setting determines the number of frames captured per second in your footage. Higher frame rates result in smoother motion and are ideal for capturing fast-moving subjects or action shots. The DJI Air 3 drone supports different frame rate options, including 24fps, 30fps, and 60fps, giving you flexibility in choosing the right frame rate for your desired look and feel.

Exposure Settings

Exposure settings control the amount of light entering the camera sensor, affecting the brightness and exposure of your images or videos. The DJI Air 3 drone offers manual exposure control, allowing you to adjust settings such as aperture, shutter speed, and ISO sensitivity to achieve the desired exposure levels. Additionally, you can use exposure compensation to fine-tune exposure settings and compensate for challenging lighting conditions.

White Balance

White balance determines the color temperature of your images or videos, ensuring accurate color reproduction under different lighting conditions. The DJI Air 3 drone offers various white balance presets, such as Sunny, Cloudy, and Indoor, as well as custom white balance settings for precise color calibration. Adjusting the white balance ensures natural-looking colors and avoids color casts or tints in your footage.

Picture Profile

Picture profiles control the color and contrast characteristics of your images or videos, allowing you to achieve a specific look or style. The DJI Air 3 drone offers different picture profiles, such as Standard, D-Cinelike, and HLG, each with unique color and contrast settings. Additionally, you can shoot in RAW format for maximum flexibility in post-processing and color grading.

Focus and Autofocus

Focus settings determine the sharpness and clarity of your images or videos by controlling the focus distance of the camera lens. The DJI Air 3 drone offers autofocus capabilities, allowing the camera to automatically adjust focus based on the subject distance and movement. Additionally, you can use manual focus for precise control over focus settings, especially when shooting stationary subjects or landscapes.

Advanced Camera Features

The DJI Air 3 drone offers advanced camera features such as HDR (High Dynamic Range), which combines multiple exposures to capture greater detail in highlights and shadows, and Pro Mode, which provides manual control over camera settings for professional-quality results. Additionally, you can use intelligent shooting modes like Time Lapse and Panorama to capture unique and creative footage.

Understanding camera settings is essential for harnessing the full potential of the DJI Air 3 drone and capturing stunning aerial footage with precision and control. By familiarizing yourself with the various camera settings available on the drone, including resolution, frame rate, exposure, white balance, picture profile, focus, and advanced features, you can customize your shooting experience and achieve professional-quality results tailored to your specific creative vision. Whether capturing cinematic video sequences, breathtaking aerial landscapes, or dynamic action shots, mastering camera settings allows you to unleash your creativity and capture compelling imagery from a unique perspective. With the DJI Air 3 drone's powerful camera capabilities and intuitive controls, you can elevate your aerial photography and videography to new heights and create captivating content that inspires and amazes.

Tips for Achieving Professional-Quality Shots

Achieving professional-quality shots with the DJI Air 3 drone requires a combination of technical know-how, creative vision, and practical skills. By following these tips and techniques, you can elevate your aerial photography and videography to the next level and capture stunning imagery that rivals the work of professional filmmakers and photographers:

1. Understand Your Equipment: Take the time to familiarize yourself with the features, functions, and capabilities of the DJI Air 3 drone, including camera settings, flight modes, and intelligent shooting modes. Knowing how to leverage your

drone's technology and controls effectively will enable you to capture better shots and achieve optimal results in various shooting scenarios.

2. Plan Your Shots: Before taking flight, plan your shots carefully by scouting locations, considering lighting conditions, and visualizing compositions. Identify points of interest, potential obstacles, and unique vantage points that will enhance your shots and add visual interest to your footage. Planning ahead will help you make the most of your flight time and capture compelling imagery with purpose and intention.

3. Optimize Camera Settings: Adjust camera settings such as resolution, frame rate, exposure, white balance, and picture profile to suit your shooting conditions and creative preferences. Experiment with different settings to achieve the desired look and feel for your shots, whether you're aiming for cinematic quality, vibrant colors, or natural tones. Pay attention to details like focus and autofocus to ensure sharp and clear images in every shot.

4. Master Flight Techniques: Develop proficiency in piloting your drone and executing smooth and controlled flight maneuvers. Practice flying in

different environments and weather conditions, mastering techniques such as hovering, ascending, descending, and navigating obstacles. Use intelligent flight modes like ActiveTrack, Waypoints, and QuickShot modes to automate complex maneuvers and capture dynamic shots with ease.

5. Frame Your Shots Thoughtfully: Compose your shots thoughtfully by considering elements such as framing, perspective, and symmetry. Use the rule of thirds to guide your composition, placing key subjects or points of interest off-center for visual interest and balance. Experiment with different angles and perspectives to capture unique viewpoints and create dynamic compositions that draw the viewer's eye.

6. Pay Attention to Lighting: Pay close attention to lighting conditions when shooting with your drone, as lighting plays a crucial role in shaping the mood, atmosphere, and overall quality of your shots. Shoot during the golden hours of sunrise and sunset for soft, warm light and long shadows that add depth and dimension to your footage. Avoid harsh midday sunlight and overcast conditions, which can result in flat, unflattering lighting.

7. Add Movement and Dynamics: Introduce movement and dynamics to your shots by incorporating camera movements, motion paths, and dynamic elements. Experiment with techniques such as panning, tilting, and tracking to add energy and excitement to your footage. Use the drone's agility and maneuverability to capture dynamic aerial perspectives and sweeping vistas that showcase the beauty and scale of your surroundings.

8. Edit and Enhance Post-Production: After capturing your shots, take the time to edit and enhance them in post-production to refine the look and feel of your footage. Use editing software to adjust color, contrast, saturation, and exposure, fine-tuning your shots for optimal visual impact. Consider adding transitions, music, and effects to enhance the storytelling and emotional resonance of your footage, creating a polished and professional final product.

9. Practice and Experiment: Continuously practice and experiment with different techniques, styles, and shooting approaches to expand your skills and creativity as a drone pilot and photographer. Embrace trial and error, learn from your mistakes, and strive for continuous improvement in your

craft. Push the boundaries of what's possible with your drone and challenge yourself to capture shots that are innovative, compelling, and visually stunning.

10. Respect Regulations and Safety: Finally, always prioritize safety and adhere to local regulations and guidelines when flying your drone. Familiarize yourself with airspace restrictions, flight limitations, and safety protocols in your area, and always fly responsibly and ethically. Respect privacy, property rights, and wildlife habitats, and prioritize the safety of yourself and others at all times.

By following these tips for achieving professional-quality shots with the DJI Air 3 drone, you can unlock the full potential of your aerial photography and videography skills and capture stunning imagery that inspires and captivates audiences. With practice, patience, and dedication, you can elevate your drone photography to new heights and create compelling visual stories that leave a lasting impression.

Using Intelligent Flight Modes for Cinematic Effects

Intelligent flight modes are powerful features available on the DJI Air 3 drone that enable users to capture cinematic effects and create visually stunning aerial footage with ease and precision. By leveraging intelligent flight modes, users can automate complex flight maneuvers, execute dynamic camera movements, and achieve professional-quality shots that rival those of Hollywood filmmakers. Let's explore how to use intelligent flight modes for cinematic effects with the DJI Air 3 drone:

Understanding Intelligent Flight Modes

Intelligent flight modes are pre-programmed flight patterns and camera movements that automate specific aerial maneuvers and creative effects, allowing users to capture cinematic shots with minimal effort and expertise. Each intelligent flight mode offers unique features and functionalities designed to enhance the creative possibilities and versatility of aerial photography and videography.

Key Intelligent Flight Modes

The DJI Air 3 drone offers a variety of intelligent flight modes, each tailored to different shooting scenarios and creative effects. Some key intelligent flight modes include:

1. ActiveTrack: ActiveTrack enables the drone to automatically track and follow a selected subject, keeping it in the frame at all times and allowing for smooth and accurate tracking shots. Users can choose from different tracking modes, such as Trace, Profile, and Spotlight, to customize the tracking behavior and achieve dynamic and engaging shots.

2. Waypoints: Waypoints allows users to plan and execute automated flight paths by defining multiple waypoints on a map interface. The drone will follow the predefined route, capturing footage or performing tasks as specified, and allowing for hands-free operation and precise control over the aircraft's trajectory and movements.

3. QuickShot Modes: QuickShot modes offer a variety of pre-programmed flight maneuvers and camera movements, such as orbits, helixes, dronies, and rocket shots, designed to capture dynamic and engaging aerial shots with ease. QuickShot modes

automate the execution of complex flight maneuvers, allowing users to focus on framing shots and capturing compelling content.

4. Point of Interest (POI): Point of Interest mode enables the drone to orbit around a selected point of interest, keeping it in the center of the frame while capturing smooth and cinematic footage. Users can adjust parameters such as altitude, radius, and speed to customize the orbiting behavior and achieve creative and dynamic shots.

Tips for Using Intelligent Flight Modes

To make the most of intelligent flight modes for cinematic effects with the DJI Air 3 drone, consider the following tips and techniques:

1. Plan Your Shots: Before using intelligent flight modes, plan your shots carefully by identifying key subjects, points of interest, and desired camera movements. Consider the creative effects you want to achieve and select the appropriate intelligent flight mode to suit your shooting goals.

2. Experiment with Settings: Experiment with different settings and parameters for intelligent flight modes, such as speed, altitude, and radius, to

achieve unique and creative effects. Adjust settings based on the specific requirements of each shot, and don't be afraid to try out different combinations to find the perfect look and feel.

3. Practice Flight Maneuvers: Practice using intelligent flight modes regularly to familiarize yourself with their capabilities and limitations. Take the time to master the controls and understand how each mode operates, ensuring smooth and precise execution of flight maneuvers and camera movements.

4. Combine Modes for Complex Shots: Combine multiple intelligent flight modes to create complex and dynamic shots with layered effects. For example, you can use ActiveTrack to follow a moving subject while orbiting around a point of interest using Point of Interest mode, resulting in dynamic and engaging footage with multiple points of focus.

5. Monitor Performance: Monitor the performance of intelligent flight modes in real time through the live video feed on the DJI Fly app or remote controller. Pay attention to framing, composition, and camera movements, making adjustments as

needed to ensure smooth and accurate execution of shots.

6. Edit and Enhance Post-Production: After capturing your shots, take the time to edit and enhance them in post-production to refine the look and feel of your footage. Use editing software to adjust color, contrast, saturation, and exposure, fine-tuning your shots for optimal visual impact.

Intelligent flight modes are powerful tools that enable users to capture cinematic effects and create visually stunning aerial footage with the DJI Air 3 drone. By leveraging features such as ActiveTrack, Waypoints, QuickShot modes, and Point of Interest, users can automate complex flight maneuvers, execute dynamic camera movements, and achieve professional-quality shots with ease and precision. By understanding how to use intelligent flight modes effectively and following best practices for planning, execution, and post-production, users can unlock the full potential of their drone and capture cinematic footage that inspires and captivates audiences. With practice, patience, and creativity, you can elevate your aerial photography and videography to new heights and create compelling visual stories that leave a lasting impression.

Chapter 7: Post-Flight Procedures

Landing and Shutting Down the Drone Safely

Landing and shutting down the drone safely is a critical aspect of responsible drone operation that ensures the well-being of the aircraft, surrounding environment, and individuals nearby. Proper landing and shutdown procedures not only protect the drone from damage but also minimize the risk of accidents or injuries during the landing process. Whether you're a beginner or an experienced drone pilot, mastering the art of safe landing and shutdown is essential for maintaining the longevity and reliability of your drone. Let's explore the steps involved in landing and shutting down the drone safely:

1. Choose a Suitable Landing Area: Before initiating the landing process, carefully select a suitable landing area that is free from obstacles, hazards, and obstructions. Choose a flat, level surface with

ample space for the drone to descend and land safely, away from trees, buildings, power lines, and other potential hazards. Avoid landing on uneven terrain, water bodies, or unstable surfaces that may pose a risk to the drone's stability and safety.

2. Descend Slowly and Gradually: Initiate the descent by reducing the throttle and descending the drone slowly and gradually towards the selected landing area. Avoid descending too quickly or aggressively, as this can lead to hard landings, bouncing, or tipping over, potentially causing damage to the drone or its components. Maintain a steady descent rate and exercise caution when approaching the ground to ensure a smooth and controlled landing.

3. Use Visual Cues for Precision: Utilize visual cues and landmarks to guide the drone's descent and maintain spatial awareness during the landing process. Keep an eye on the drone's altitude, distance from the ground, and alignment with the landing area, using the drone's onboard camera feed or line of sight for reference. Adjust the descent speed and trajectory as needed to ensure precise positioning and alignment with the landing spot.

4. Engage Landing Gear (if applicable): If your drone is equipped with landing gear, activate it before touching down to provide additional stability and support during the landing process. Lower the landing gear gradually as the drone approaches the ground, ensuring that it makes contact with the surface smoothly and evenly. Avoid abrupt or forceful deployment of the landing gear, as this can cause instability or damage to the drone's frame or landing gear mechanism.

5. Execute Soft Touchdown: As the drone descends towards the landing area, aim for a soft and gentle touchdown to minimize impact and prevent damage to the drone or its components. Reduce the throttle gradually as the drone approaches the ground, allowing it to settle gently onto the surface without bouncing or jolting. Maintain control of the drone until it comes to a complete stop, ensuring that it remains upright and stable after landing.

6. Power Down the Motors: Once the drone has landed safely, power down the motors to shut down the aircraft and deactivate the propellers. Depending on your drone model, you can use the remote controller or the onboard controls to initiate the shutdown sequence. Follow the manufacturer's instructions and guidelines for powering down the

drone safely, ensuring that all propellers come to a complete stop before proceeding.

7. Disconnect Battery and Fold Arms (if applicable): After shutting down the drone, disconnect the battery to prevent accidental activation and conserve power for future flights. If your drone features foldable arms or collapsible design, fold them in securely to minimize the risk of damage during transport or storage. Check for any loose or damaged components and perform a visual inspection to ensure that the drone is in good condition before packing it away.

8. Secure and Store the Drone: Once the drone has been landed and shut down safely, secure it in a protective case or storage bag to prevent damage during transport or storage. Store the drone in a cool, dry place away from direct sunlight, moisture, or extreme temperatures to preserve its functionality and longevity. Follow the manufacturer's recommendations for maintenance and storage to keep your drone in optimal condition between flights.

Landing and shutting down the drone safely is an essential skill for drone pilots of all levels, ensuring the safe operation and longevity of the aircraft. By following proper landing procedures, exercising caution during descent, and executing a soft touchdown, you can minimize the risk of damage to the drone and surrounding environment. Additionally, powering down the motors, disconnecting the battery, and securing the drone for transport or storage are crucial steps in maintaining the integrity and reliability of the aircraft. By mastering the art of safe landing and shutdown, you can enjoy countless hours of safe and enjoyable drone flying while preserving the longevity and performance of your drone for years to come.

Maintenance Tips for Prolonging the Drone's Lifespan

Maintenance is crucial for prolonging the lifespan of your drone and ensuring its continued performance and reliability throughout its operational life. By implementing regular maintenance practices and following manufacturer guidelines, you can minimize wear and tear, prevent damage, and extend the longevity of your drone. Here are some essential maintenance tips for keeping your drone in top condition:

1. Pre-flight Inspection: Perform a thorough pre-flight inspection before each flight to check for any signs of damage, wear, or malfunction. Inspect the drone's exterior for cracks, dents, or scratches, and ensure that all components are securely attached and functioning properly. Check the propellers for damage or signs of wear and replace any damaged or worn-out propellers before flying.

2. Cleanliness: Keep your drone clean and free from dirt, dust, and debris that can accumulate during flights. Use a soft brush or compressed air to remove debris from the drone's exterior, motors, and vents, paying particular attention to the camera lens and gimbal. Avoid using harsh chemicals or abrasive materials that may damage the drone's finish or components.

3. Battery Care: Proper battery care is essential for maintaining the longevity and performance of your drone's batteries. Follow manufacturer guidelines for charging, storing, and handling batteries, and avoid overcharging or discharging them excessively. Store batteries in a cool, dry place away from direct

sunlight and extreme temperatures, and inspect them regularly for signs of swelling or damage.

4. Firmware Updates: Stay up to date with firmware updates released by the drone manufacturer to ensure optimal performance and compatibility with the latest features and functionalities. Regularly check for firmware updates through the manufacturer's official website or mobile app and follow the instructions for installing updates safely and correctly.

5. Motor Maintenance: Inspect the drone's motors regularly for signs of wear, damage, or debris that may affect their performance. Clean the motor shafts and bearings with a soft brush or compressed air to remove dirt and debris, and lubricate them as needed according to manufacturer recommendations. Replace worn-out or damaged motors promptly to prevent further damage to the drone.

6. Gimbal Calibration: Calibrate the drone's gimbal regularly to ensure smooth and stable camera performance during flights. Follow the manufacturer's instructions for gimbal calibration and perform the calibration process in a flat, stable environment free from interference. Check the

gimbal's range of motion and stability after calibration to ensure proper alignment and functionality.

7. Propeller Maintenance: Inspect the drone's propellers for damage, wear, or imbalance before each flight, and replace any damaged or worn-out propellers promptly. Clean the propellers regularly to remove dirt, dust, and debris that may affect their performance, and ensure that they are securely attached and balanced before takeoff.

8. Storage: Store your drone in a protective case or storage bag when not in use to protect it from dust, moisture, and physical damage. Choose a cool, dry location away from direct sunlight and extreme temperatures for storing your drone, and avoid storing it in areas prone to humidity or moisture buildup.

9. Post-flight Inspection: After each flight, inspect the drone for any signs of damage or wear that may have occurred during operation. Check for loose or damaged components, debris in the motors or propellers, and any abnormalities in the drone's performance or behavior. Address any issues promptly and perform necessary maintenance or repairs to keep your drone in optimal condition.

10. Professional Servicing: If you encounter any issues or problems with your drone that you are unable to resolve on your own, seek professional servicing from authorized repair centers or technicians. Avoid attempting DIY repairs or modifications that may void the drone's warranty or cause further damage, and always consult with the manufacturer or a qualified technician for guidance and assistance.

Regular maintenance is essential for prolonging the lifespan of your drone and ensuring its continued performance and reliability over time. By following these maintenance tips and practices, you can minimize wear and tear, prevent damage, and extend the longevity of your drone for years to come. Incorporate regular maintenance into your drone flying routine and prioritize proper care and upkeep to maximize the lifespan and enjoyment of your drone.

Chapter 8: Troubleshooting and FAQs

While drones offer incredible capabilities and versatility, they are not immune to technical issues or malfunctions. Understanding common issues and knowing how to troubleshoot them is essential for drone pilots to ensure smooth and trouble-free operation. Here are some common issues drone pilots may encounter and troubleshooting steps to address them:

GPS Signal Loss

Issue: One of the most common issues drone pilots face is loss of GPS signal, which can lead to loss of position accuracy, navigation difficulties, and even flyaways.

Troubleshooting Steps

- Ensure the drone is in an open area with a clear line of sight to the sky.
- Check for nearby sources of interference such as tall buildings, trees, or electromagnetic fields.

- Reboot the drone and remote controller and wait for the GPS signal to reacquire.
- Calibrate the drone's compass and GPS system according to manufacturer instructions.
- Update firmware and software to the latest versions to improve GPS performance.

Motor or Propeller Issues

Issue: Drones may experience motor or propeller issues such as motor failure, propeller damage, or imbalance, which can affect flight stability and performance.

Troubleshooting Steps

- Inspect motors and propellers for signs of damage, wear, or debris.
- Replace damaged or worn-out propellers with new ones.
- Clean debris from motors and propellers using a soft brush or compressed air.
- Ensure propellers are securely attached and balanced before flight.
- Calibrate motor and propeller settings in the drone's software if necessary.

Gimbal Malfunction

Issue: The gimbal, which stabilizes the camera during flight, may experience malfunctions such as drifting, vibration, or erratic movements.

Troubleshooting Steps

- Check for physical damage or obstruction to the gimbal and camera.
- Calibrate the gimbal according to manufacturer instructions to reset its position and stability.
- Ensure the drone is on a flat, stable surface when calibrating the gimbal.
- Update firmware and software to the latest versions to address known gimbal issues.

Battery Issues

Issue: Drone batteries may experience issues such as poor performance, short flight times, or sudden power loss during flight.

Troubleshooting Steps

- Check battery connections and ensure they are secure and free from corrosion.

- Calibrate the battery level indicator in the drone's software to improve accuracy.
- Monitor battery voltage and temperature during flight and land the drone safely if levels drop too low.
- Store batteries properly in a cool, dry place and avoid overcharging or discharging them excessively.

Connectivity Problems

Issue: Drones may experience connectivity problems between the drone and remote controller, leading to loss of control or signal dropout.

Troubleshooting Steps

- Ensure the remote controller and drone are properly paired and within range.
- Check for sources of interference such as Wi-Fi networks, radio signals, or electronic devices.
- Reboot the drone and remote controller and wait for them to reconnect.
- Update firmware and software to the latest versions to improve connectivity and compatibility.

Software Glitches

Issue: Drones may experience software glitches or bugs that affect performance, stability, or functionality.

Troubleshooting Steps

- Reboot the drone and remote controller to reset the software and clear temporary glitches.
- Update firmware and software to the latest versions to address known issues and bugs.
- Reset factory settings or reinstall the drone's software if necessary.
- Contact manufacturer support for assistance if issues persist or worsen.

Being aware of common issues and knowing how to troubleshoot them is essential for drone pilots to ensure safe and smooth operation of their aircraft. By following these troubleshooting steps and best practices, drone pilots can address common issues quickly and effectively, minimizing downtime and maximizing their flying experience. Additionally, staying informed about firmware updates, maintenance procedures, and manufacturer recommendations can help prevent issues from occurring and ensure optimal performance of your drone over time.

Answers to Frequently Asked Questions

Frequently Asked Questions (FAQs) provide valuable insights and solutions to common queries that drone pilots encounter during their flying adventures. Here are answers to some of the most frequently asked questions about drone operation, maintenance, and troubleshooting:

How do I choose the right drone for my needs?

Answer: Choosing the right drone depends on your specific needs, preferences, and budget. Consider factors such as flight time, camera quality, flight range, and advanced features like obstacle avoidance and GPS tracking. Research different drone models, read reviews, and compare specifications to find the one that best suits your requirements.

Do I need to register my drone with the aviation authorities?

Answer: In many countries, drones above a certain weight threshold need to be registered with aviation authorities before they can be flown legally. Check the regulations in your country or region to determine if registration is required and follow the necessary steps to register your drone if applicable.

How do I improve the battery life of my drone?

Answer: To improve battery life, avoid overcharging or discharging the battery excessively, as this can shorten its lifespan. Store batteries properly in a cool, dry place when not in use and follow manufacturer guidelines for charging and maintenance. Consider purchasing additional batteries to extend your flying time without waiting for recharging.

What should I do if my drone crashes?

Answer: If your drone crashes, assess the damage and inspect the aircraft for any signs of damage or malfunction. Check for broken propellers, damaged components, or loose connections, and address any issues before attempting to fly again. Follow manufacturer guidelines for troubleshooting and repair or contact customer support for assistance if needed.

How do I capture smooth and stable footage with my drone?

Answer: To capture smooth and stable footage, ensure your drone is equipped with a gimbal-stabilized camera and use features like GPS stabilization and intelligent flight modes to assist with smooth flying and camera movements. Avoid flying in windy conditions or turbulent weather, and practice gentle and precise control inputs to minimize shaking or vibration in your footage.

Can I fly my drone in restricted airspace or near airports?

Answer: No, it is illegal and unsafe to fly drones in restricted airspace or near airports, as it poses a risk to manned aircraft and violates aviation regulations. Always check for airspace restrictions and adhere to local laws and regulations when flying your drone. Use tools like airspace maps and mobile apps to identify restricted areas and plan your flights accordingly.

How do I maintain and care for my drone?

Answer: Regular maintenance is essential for prolonging the lifespan and performance of your drone. Clean the aircraft regularly to remove dirt, dust, and debris, and inspect components for signs of wear or damage. Follow manufacturer guidelines for battery care, firmware updates, and storage to ensure optimal performance and reliability.

What should I do if I encounter interference or signal loss during flight?

Answer: If you encounter interference or signal loss during flight, remain calm and attempt to regain control of the drone by adjusting the remote controller's position or altitude. Move to a different location away from potential sources of interference and wait for the signal to stabilize. Avoid making abrupt control inputs or panic maneuvers that may exacerbate the situation.

Can I fly my drone at night or in low light conditions?

Answer: Flying drones at night or in low light conditions can be challenging and may pose safety risks, especially if you lose visual contact with the aircraft. Check local regulations regarding nighttime flying and ensure your drone is equipped with adequate lighting or night flight capabilities if flying in low light conditions. Exercise caution and prioritize safety when flying in challenging lighting conditions.

How do I become a certified drone pilot?

To become a certified drone pilot, you may need to undergo training and certification from aviation authorities or accredited training organizations. Research the requirements and regulations in your country or region for drone pilot certification and follow the necessary steps to obtain certification if required. Complete any required training courses, exams, or practical assessments to demonstrate your competence and knowledge as a drone pilot.

Frequently Asked Questions (FAQs) provide valuable guidance and solutions to common queries that drone pilots encounter during their flying adventures. By addressing common concerns about drone operation, maintenance, troubleshooting, and regulations, pilots can enhance their knowledge and confidence to enjoy safe and rewarding drone flying experiences. Stay informed, follow best practices, and continue learning to maximize your enjoyment and proficiency as a drone pilot.

Dear Reader,

I hope you enjoyed reading this book as much as I enjoyed writing it. Your feedback is incredibly valuable, not only to me but also to other potential readers. If you found the book insightful, entertaining, or helpful, I would greatly appreciate it if you could take a moment to leave an honest review on Amazon.

Your reviews contribute to the book's visibility and help fellow readers make informed decisions. Whether it's a few words or a more detailed review, your thoughts really matter.

Thank you for being part of this literary journey. I appreciate your time and feedback.

Best regards,

Kevin Editions

www.ingramcontent.com/pod-product-compliance
Lightning Source LLC
LaVergne TN
LVHW051714050326
832903LV00032B/4193